Stories of Jesus

Story adaptation by
Sarah Toast

Illustrations by
Gary Torrisi

Louis Weber, C.E.O.
Publications International, Ltd.
7373 North Cicero Avenue
Lincolnwood, Illinois 60646

Manufactured in U.S.A.

8 7 6 5 4 3 2 1

ISBN: 0-7853-2223-X

PUBLICATIONS INTERNATIONAL, LTD.
Rainbow is a trademark of Publications International, Ltd.

Jesus often taught by telling parables. A parable is a story about an everyday situation that teaches a special lesson. Jesus hoped people would remember his teachings and think about their meaning.

Jesus went through one town and village after another, teaching the people. One day some townspeople complained about Jesus because he taught people who had broken rules. Jesus answered them by telling a parable about God's love and forgiveness for someone who is sorry for making a mistake.

Mrs. Blanchard

Many years ago, there was a man who had two sons. The younger son was tired of living at home and having to work hard on the family farm. One day he said to his father, "Father, I want my share of what you have that would be mine someday."

The father gave the younger son a share of the family property. A few days after this happened, the son gathered up all of his belongings and left the family farm to travel to a country that was very far away.

When he arrived in a distant town, the younger son found many new friends and spent his money freely on whatever he wanted.

All too soon he had no money left. All the money his father had given him was gone. When he went to his new friends to see if they would help him, they were nowhere to be found.

To make matters worse, the crops failed in that country, and food was very hard to find. The younger son could find nothing to eat.

The son was so needy that he finally took a job tending pigs. This was not a very good job, but he was desperate and it was all he could do.

Still, no one would give him food. The son was so hungry that he would gladly have eaten the pigs' food!

Then the son remembered how good the food was back at his family's home and how well even the hired workers on his father's farm ate. He decided that he would return home and beg for his father to forgive him.

The younger son set off to return to his father. He hoped his father would take him in as a servant.

While he approached his family's home, the father saw his younger son and felt pity for him. The father ran to his son, put his arms around him, and kissed him.

The son said, "Father, I have done you wrong. I am no longer worthy to be your son." But then the father called for a huge feast to celebrate the return of his younger son.

The older son heard the music, and he came back from the fields where he was working. He was angry with his father for giving a feast for the son who had gone away and wasted all his money.

"For all these years I have worked for you, and I have never disobeyed you, yet you have never given me anything," said the older son.

The father replied, "Son, it is right to celebrate, because your brother was as good as dead, and now he is back home. He was lost and now is found."

Jesus told the townspeople another parable to explain the meaning of God's commandment to love your neighbor.

A man was walking down the road from Jerusalem to Jericho. His donkeys were loaded up with his belongings.

Some robbers hid behind the rocks. They attacked the traveler and stole all he had, even his clothes. They beat him and left him in the road.

Later a priest came along. He saw the injured man but did not stop. A man from the temple also walked past.

Then a foreigner came along, a man from Samaria. The Samaritan pitied the injured man. He cleaned and bandaged his wounds. He poured oil on them to make them feel better. Then he gently lifted the injured man onto his donkey and he took him to the first inn that they could find.

The good Samaritan rented a room for the two of them to sleep in during the night. The Samaritan stayed with the injured man and did everything he could think of to take care of him.

The next day, the Samaritan had to go. But he did not want to leave the injured man. He gave the innkeeper money to care for him. "Take care of him," said the Samaritan. "If you have to spend more, I will repay you when I return."

After telling the story of the injured man and the good Samaritan who helped him, Jesus asked his listener, "Which of these three men showed love to the poor man who was robbed and then beaten?" His listener answered, "The one who took care of him."

Jesus told his listener, "You should be like that."

Jesus taught people to help those in need, even those who are different, just as the Samaritan helped someone from Jerusalem. We are all neighbors.